MW00442579

The First
NIGHT BEFORE CHRISTMAS

By

Daniel F. Wiegand

Copyright @ 2021 by Daniel F. Wiegand

All Rights Reserved

No part of this publication may be reproduced or transmitted, in any form or by any means, electronic, mechanical, photocopying, recording, or otherwise, without the written permission of the author.

First published by DFW Publications, LLC Waterford, MI

Illustrated by Carina Reytblat of Israel, as a work for hire through Fiverr.

Printed in the United States of America

ISBN: 978-1-7376479-3-5 (hardcover)

Dedication

This book is dedicated with love to my grandchildren, Elizabeth, Kadin, Haley, Matthew, Paul and Andrew.

'Twas the night before Christmas, and all through the town,
It was crowded with people from all around.

Joseph and Mary had come a long way.
They desperately needed a good place to stay.

"I'm sorry" was all the Innkeeper could say.
"All I have is the manger out back and some hay."

"I'll take it" said Joseph as he paid for the night.
"Don't worry" said Mary, "God makes all things right."

With the cattle and other farm animals around,
Joseph made a bed out of straw on the ground.

And there in the midst of those humble beginnings,
A child was born who would be King of Kings.

Wise men came and angels appeared,

But the little boy's power by Herod was feared.

The Holy Family had to escape.
They fled down to Egypt until it was safe.

Jesus grew to a man,

But he lives on today to save all who are lost.

**And so in the midst of this blessed Christmas season,
Let's not forget the Lord's birth is its reason.**

His is the greatest gift we can receive.
It's eternal life for all who believe.

So thank God this night for a comfortable bed.

Thank him for the roof you have over your head.

And pray for those who don't have these things.

As it was that first Christmas for the King of all Kings.